Transitioning SQL to dplyr
For R Users

Djoni Darmawikarta

Table of Contents

Acknowledgements

Thanks to the R Core Team and Hadley Wickham and Romain Francois.

R Core Team (2015). R: A language and environment for statistical computing. R Foundation for Statistical Computing, Vienna, Austria. URL http://www.R-project.org/

Hadley Wickham and Romain Francois (2016). dplyr: A Grammar of Data Manipulation. R package version 0.5.0. http://CRAN.R-project.org/package=dplyr

Preface

Welcome to *Transitioning SQL to dplyr*.

If you are an R user who wants to move away from SQL and instead wants to manipulate data using the R's dplyr functions, then this book is perfect for you.

dplyr is an R package available for download from the CRAN website, https://cran.r-project.org

You will learn the dplyr's equivalents of the SQL's DML statements (Data Manipulation Language): the SELECT, INSERT, UPDATE, and DELETE statements.[1]

Prerequisite

This book teaches you neither R nor SQL; you should already have some R and SQL working skill.[2]

---

[1] If you want to use SQL inside R, read my book "R Data Preparation and Manipulation Using the sqldf Package: Executing SQL Statements from Within R Program"

[2] I published a few SQL books, such as "Oracle SQL". You can buy them from Amazon online book stores.

Chapter 1: SQL vs dplyr

All SQL queries use the SELECT statement. The SELECT statement has the following syntax.

```
SELECT columns FROM table WHERE condition ORDER BY
      columns;
```

The dplyr equivalent is as follows.

```
select(data frame, columns) %>% filter(condition) %>%
      arrange(columns)
```

The select, filter, and arrange, are functions. The %>% (a.k.a. pipe) feeds the output data from its left-side function to the right-side function.

Let's look at an example.

Assume we have the following hec data frame.[3]

```
> hec
    source  hair    eye gender freq
1       Fi Brown  Brown   Male   53
2       Fi   Red  Brown   Male   10
3       Un Blond  Brown   Male    3
4       Fi Black   Blue   Male   11
5       Kp Blond   Blue Female   30
6       Fi Black  Hazel   Male   10
7       Un Brown  Hazel   Male   25
8       Kp   Red  Hazel   Male    7
9       Kp Black  Black   Male    3
10      Bl Brown  Green   Male   15
11      Bl   Red  Green Female    7
12      Bl Blond  Brown Female    4
13      Un Black   Blue Female    9
14      Un   Red  Hazel Female    7
```

If you want to select the hair column (hair colour) with freq (frequency) greater than or equal to 10, and order the output rows by the hair, you'd run a SQL statement like the following. (Assuming we have a similar hec relational table with the same data)

```
SELECT hair FROM hec WHERE n >= 50 ORDER BY hair;
```

---

[3] You will learn about this hec table in Chapter 2.

The dplyr equivalent is as follows.

```
> select(hec, hair, freq) %>%
filter(freq >= 10) %>% arrange
(hair)
     hair freq
1 Black    11
2 Black    10
3 Blond    30
4 Brown    53
5 Brown    25
6 Brown    15
7   Red    10
```

Saving the Output

The select, and other dplyr functions for that matter, does not change the data frame.

```
> select(hec, hair, freq) %>%
+ filter(freq >= 10) %>%
+ arrange(hair)
    hair freq
1 Black    11
2 Black    10
3 Blond    30
4 Brown    53
5 Brown    25
6 Brown    15
7   Red    10
> hec
    source  hair    eye gender freq
1       Fi Brown  Brown   Male   53
2       Fi   Red  Brown   Male   10
3       Un Blond  Brown   Male    3
4       Fi Black   Blue   Male   11
5       Kp Blond   Blue Female   30
6       Fi Black  Hazel   Male   10
7       Un Brown  Hazel   Male   25
8       Kp   Red  Hazel   Male    7
9       Kp Black  Black   Male    3
10      Bl Brown  Green   Male   15
11      Bl   Red  Green Female    7
12      Bl Blond  Brown Female    4
13      Un Black   Blue Female    9
14      Un   Red  Hazel Female    7
```

If you need to preserve the output, you need to save it. The following saves the result of the previous example into another data frame.

```
> result1 <- select(hec, hair, freq) %>%
+ filter(freq >= 10) %>%
+ arrange(hair)
> result1
    hair freq
1 Black    11
2 Black    10
3 Blond    30
4 Brown    53
5 Brown    25
6 Brown    15
7   Red    10
```

Case sensitivity

While SQL statement is case insensitive, dplyr is case sensitive.

```
Select (dataframe, columns)
```

As the select function must be in lowercases, with the s in uppercase, the function will not run.

```
> Select (hec, Hair, n)
Error: could not find function "Select"
```

Loading the dplyr

As you will use its functions you should load the dplyr package.

```
> library(dplyr)
```

Chapter 2: Book Examples

The data set uses in the examples are intentionally small to facilitate easier learning/visual inspection on the print of this book.

hec dataframe

The examples in this book use the following hec and hec_source dataframes.

```
> hec
    source  hair    eye gender freq
1       Fi Brown  Brown   Male   53
2       Fi   Red  Brown   Male   10
3       Un Blond  Brown   Male    3
4       Fi Black   Blue   Male   11
5       Kp Blond   Blue Female   30
6       Fi Black  Hazel   Male   10
7       Un Brown  Hazel   Male   25
8       Kp   Red  Hazel   Male    7
9       Kp Black  Black   Male    3
10      Bl Brown  Green   Male   15
11      Bl   Red  Green Female    7
12      Bl Blond  Brown Female    4
13      Un Black   Blue Female    9
14      Un   Red  Hazel Female    7
```

```
> hec_source
  source source.name
1     Fi        Finch
2     Kp      Kipling
3     Un        Union
4     Bl Yonge Bloor
```

Other data frames will be introduced later as required in specific chapters.

Chapter 3: Extracting Rows

In SQL you extract rows using the WHERE condition. In SQL extracting rows are more known as "querying data".

```
SELECT columns WHERE condition;
```

In dplyr you use the filter function.

```
filter(dataframe, condition)
```

Here is an example to select Brown eye rows.

```
> filter(hec, eye == 'Brown')
  source  hair    eye gender freq
1     Fi Brown  Brown   Male   53
2     Fi   Red  Brown   Male   10
3     Un Blond  Brown   Male    3
4     Bl Blond  Brown Female    4
```

Comparison operators

In addition to the equality (==) comparison you can also apply other logical comparisons, such as < (less than), > (greater than), <= (less than or equal to), >= (greater than or equal to).

Here's an example using the >= comparison.

```
> filter(hec, freq >= 25)
  source  hair    eye gender freq
1     Fi Brown  Brown   Male   53
2     Kp Blond   Blue Female   30
3     Un Brown  Hazel   Male   25
```

Compound Condition

You can form a compound condition using the Boolean operators & (and) and | (or). Here is an example using &.

```
> filter(hec, eye == 'Brown' &
+ gender == 'Male')
  source  hair    eye gender freq
1     Fi Brown  Brown   Male   53
2     Fi   Red  Brown   Male   10
3     Un Blond  Brown   Male    3
```

Another example using | is as follows.

```
> filter(hec, eye == 'Brown' |
+ hair == 'Black')
  source  hair    eye gender freq
1     Fi Brown  Brown   Male   53
2     Fi   Red  Brown   Male   10
3     Un Blond  Brown   Male    3
4     Fi Black   Blue   Male   11
5     Fi Black  Hazel   Male   10
6     Kp Black  Black   Male    3
7     Bl Blond  Brown Female    4
8     Un Black   Blue Female    9
```

xor (Exclusive Or)

Another Boolean operator you can use is the xor (exclusive or)

The following example will select rows of Brown eye, rows of Male rows, but not rows of Brown eye and Male.

```
> filter(hec, xor(eye == 'Brown',
+ gender == 'Male'))
  source  hair    eye gender freq
1     Fi Black   Blue   Male   11
2     Fi Black  Hazel   Male   10
3     Un Brown  Hazel   Male   25
4     Kp   Red  Hazel   Male    7
5     Kp Black  Black   Male    3
6     Bl Brown  Green   Male   15
7     Bl Blond  Brown Female    4
```

Parentheses

Similar to that in SQL, you can control the precedence of the logical evaluation in a compound condition by parenthesizing the parts.

The following does not use any parenthesis. The & is evaluated first.

```
> filter(hec, eye == 'Brown' |
+ hair == 'Blond' &
+ gender == 'Female')
  source  hair    eye gender freq
1     Fi Brown Brown   Male   53
2     Fi   Red Brown   Male   10
3     Un Blond Brown   Male    3
4     Kp Blond  Blue Female   30
5     Bl Blond Brown Female    4
```

Now, we put the OR in parentheses. As a result, only Female is in the output.

```
> filter(hec, (eye == 'Brown' |
+ hair == 'Blond') &
+ gender == 'Female')
  source  hair    eye gender freq
1     Kp Blond  Blue Female   30
2     Bl Blond Brown Female    4
```

NOT

The NOT is similar to that in SQL. You use the NOT operator (!) to negate a condition. Here is an example which select rows where the eye color is not Black or gender is not Male.

```
> filter(hec, ! (eye == 'Black' |
+ gender == 'Male'))
  source hair    eye gender freq
1     Kp Blond  Blue Female   30
2     Bl   Red Green Female    7
3     Bl Blond Brown Female    4
4     Un Black  Blue Female    9
5     Un   Red Hazel Female    7
```

Distinct Rows

In SQL, we use the DISTINCT in the SELECT statement.

```
SELECT DISTINCT(columns) FROM table;
```

In dplyr, we use the distinct function function (not the select function) to remove duplicate rows. Here is an example where we want only distinct hair color.

```
> distinct(hec, hair)
    hair
1 Brown
2   Red
3 Blond
4 Black
```

Distinct on multiple columns

You can select distinct rows on more than one column. The following select distinct rows on the gender and eye combinations.

```
> distinct(hec, eye, gender)
    eye gender
1 Brown   Male
2  Blue   Male
3  Blue Female
4 Hazel   Male
5 Black   Male
6 Green   Male
7 Green Female
8 Brown Female
9 Hazel Female
```

%in%

In SQL, you use IN operator to list values as a condition to match in selecting rows.

```
SELECT columns FROM table WHERE column IN(values);
```

Similarly, the %in% in dplyr allows you to select by a list of values. You can form the list of values using the c vector creation function, as demonstrated in the following example where we form a list of Green and Blue.

```
> filter(hec, eye %in%
+ c('Green', 'Blue'))
  source  hair   eye gender freq
1     Fi Black  Blue   Male   11
2     Kp Blond  Blue Female   30
3     Bl Brown Green   Male   15
4     Bl   Red Green Female    7
5     Un Black  Blue Female    9
```

Here is another example, where we compound the %in% with an AND (&) to select Male with Green or Blue eyes.

```
> filter(hec, eye %in%
+ c('Green', 'Blue') &
+ gender == 'Male')
  source  hair   eye gender freq
1     Fi Black  Blue   Male   11
2     Bl Brown Green   Male   15
```

between

To select based on a range of values, just like in SQL, we use between. Here is an example to get rows with n between 20 and 50 inclusive.

```
> filter(hec, between(freq, 20, 50))
  source  hair    eye gender freq
1     Kp Blond  Blue Female   30
2     Un Brown Hazel   Male   25
```

As another example, the following has an additional condition, which is an equality condition further restricting the output to Male only.

```
> filter(hec, between(freq, 20, 50) &
+ gender == 'Male')
  source  hair    eye gender freq
1     Un Brown Hazel   Male   25
```

Regular Expression

Some SQL implementations, such as Oracle, support selecting rows using regular expression in the condition. You can similarly use the grepl in dplyr to search by regular expression.

Here is a simple example to search rows with R as the first character in the hair, which is only Red.

```
> filter(hec, grepl("R.", hair))
  source hair    eye gender freq
1     Fi  Red  Brown   Male   10
2     Kp  Red  Hazel   Male    7
3     Bl  Red  Green Female    7
4     Un  Red  Hazel Female    7
```

Here's another with a bit more complex pattern of the regular expression. The pattern is to search hair color that starts with an uppercase character of A, B, C, followed by lowercase character of l, m, ...o. Only Black and Blond qualify.

```
> filter(hec, grepl("[A-C][l-o]", hair))
  source  hair    eye gender freq
1     Un Blond  Brown   Male    3
2     Fi Black   Blue   Male   11
3     Kp Blond   Blue Female   30
4     Fi Black  Hazel   Male   10
5     Kp Black  Black   Male    3
6     Bl Blond  Brown Female    4
7     Un Black   Blue Female    9
```

You need to know how to form the patterns of regular expression for constructing much more complex search argument of the grepl; and, there's more helper than the grepl supported by the dplyr.

NULL Handling

The equivalent of SQL's NULL (missing value) in R is NA.

Let's add a row into hec with NA except for the hair.

```
> hec <- add_row(hec, hair = 'Blond')
> hec
     source  hair    eye gender freq
1        Fi Brown  Brown   Male   53
2        Fi   Red  Brown   Male   10
3        Un Blond  Brown   Male    3
4        Fi Black   Blue   Male   11
5        Kp Blond   Blue Female   30
6        Fi Black  Hazel   Male   10
7        Un Brown  Hazel   Male   25
8        Kp   Red  Hazel   Male    7
9        Kp Black  Black   Male    3
10       Bl Brown  Green   Male   15
11       Bl   Red  Green Female    7
12       Bl Blond  Brown Female    4
13       Un Black   Blue Female    9
14       Un   Red  Hazel Female    7
15     <NA> Blond   <NA>   <NA>   NA
```

While in SQL we use IS NULL in the WHERE condition to test if a column is null

```
SELECT columns FROM table WHERE column IS NULL;
```

in dplyr, we use is.na, like the following.

```
> filter(hec, is.na(eye))
  source  hair  eye gender freq
1   <NA> Blond <NA>   <NA>   NA
```

Top/Bottom Rows

Selecting Top Rows

The top_n function(data.frame, n, wt) gives us the top n rows ordered by wt, which defaults to the last column if we don't specify wt.

In the following example we request top 14 rows as ordered by the freq column.

```
> top_n(hec, 5, freq)
  source  hair    eye gender freq
1      Fi Brown Brown    Male   53
2      Fi Black  Blue    Male   11
3      Kp Blond  Blue  Female   30
4      Un Brown Hazel    Male   25
5      Bl Brown Green    Male   15
```

Duplicate ranks

If we request top 6, we will get 7 rows, as hec has three rows with freq = 10, as duplicate rows (have the same freq) covered by n are taken by the top_n function.

```
> top_n(hec, 6, freq)
  source  hair    eye gender freq
1      Fi Brown Brown    Male   53
2      Fi   Red Brown    Male   10
3      Fi Black  Blue    Male   11
4      Kp Blond  Blue  Female   30
5      Fi Black Hazel    Male   10
6      Un Brown Hazel    Male   25
7      Bl Brown Green    Male   15
```

Last column default

Actually we don't need to specify freq in the previous examples, as the top_n function by default is order by the last column of the data frame and freq is the last column of our hec data frame.

```
> top_n(hec, 6)
Selecting by freq
  source  hair    eye gender freq
1     Fi Brown  Brown   Male   53
2     Fi   Red  Brown   Male   10
3     Fi Black   Blue   Male   11
4     Kp Blond   Blue Female   30
5     Fi Black  Hazel   Male   10
6     Un Brown  Hazel   Male   25
7     Bl Brown  Green   Male   15
```

Bottom Rows

To get the n bottom rows, you specify -n (prefix with a minus) as shown in the following example.

```
> top_n(hec, -4)
Selecting by freq
  source  hair    eye gender freq
1      Un Blond Brown    Male    3
2      Kp   Red Hazel    Male    7
3      Kp Black Black    Male    3
4      Bl   Red Green Female    7
5      Bl Blond Brown Female    4
6      Un   Red Hazel Female    7
```

Note that the NA row is excluded from the ranking.

By Row Position

Use the slice function(data.frame, positions) function to select row(s) by their positions.

Here's again the hec for your reference.

```
> hec
    source  hair    eye gender freq
1       Fi Brown  Brown   Male   53
2       Fi   Red  Brown   Male   10
3       Un Blond  Brown   Male    3
4       Fi Black   Blue   Male   11
5       Kp Blond   Blue Female   30
6       Fi Black  Hazel   Male   10
7       Un Brown  Hazel   Male   25
8       Kp   Red  Hazel   Male    7
9       Kp Black  Black   Male    3
10      Bl Brown  Green   Male   15
11      Bl   Red  Green Female    7
12      Bl Blond  Brown Female    4
13      Un Black   Blue Female    9
14      Un   Red  Hazel Female    7
15    <NA> Blond   <NA>   <NA>   NA
```

The following example selects row 1 to 5.

```
> slice(hec, 1:5)
  source  hair    eye gender freq
1     Fi Brown  Brown   Male   53
2     Fi   Red  Brown   Male   10
3     Un Blond  Brown   Male    3
4     Fi Black   Blue   Male   11
5     Kp Blond   Blue Female   30
```

And the following extracts row 5, 10, and 15 only.

```
> slice(hec, c(5, 10, 15))
  source  hair    eye gender freq
1     Kp Blond   Blue Female   30
2     Bl Brown  Green   Male   15
3   <NA> Blond   <NA>   <NA>   NA
```

Chapter 4: Selecting Columns

In SQL, to select one or more columns, you use the SELECT statement and list columns in the SELECT clause.

```
SELECT columns FROM table
```

In dplyr, you use the select function as follows.

```
select(dataframe, columns)
```

The following selects the eye, gender, and freq columns of the Male rows.

```
> select(hec, eye, gender, freq)
     eye gender freq
1  Brown   Male   53
2  Brown   Male   10
3  Brown   Male    3
4   Blue   Male   11
5   Blue Female   30
6  Hazel   Male   10
7  Hazel   Male   25
8  Hazel   Male    7
9  Black   Male    3
10 Green   Male   15
11 Green Female    7
12 Brown Female    4
13  Blue Female    9
14 Hazel Female    7
15  <NA>   <NA>   NA
```

You sequence the columns in the select's parameters as you want to see them in the output. The following same three output columns are listed in the parameters in a different sequence: gender, then freq, then eye.

```
> select(hec, gender, freq, eye)
   gender freq    eye
1    Male   53 Brown
2    Male   10 Brown
3    Male    3 Brown
4    Male   11  Blue
5  Female   30  Blue
6    Male   10 Hazel
7    Male   25 Hazel
8    Male    7 Hazel
9    Male    3 Black
10   Male   15 Green
11 Female    7 Green
12 Female    4 Brown
13 Female    9  Blue
14 Female    7 Hazel
15   <NA>   NA  <NA>
```

De-selecting Columns

The select function has a feature allowing you to de-select column(s). This feature is especially useful when your data frame has many columns and you want most of them (not all).

In the following function we want to select all columns, except the gender column.

```
> select(hec, - gender)
   source  hair    eye freq
1      Fi Brown  Brown   53
2      Fi   Red  Brown   10
3      Un Blond  Brown    3
4      Fi Black   Blue   11
5      Kp Blond   Blue   30
6      Fi Black  Hazel   10
7      Un Brown  Hazel   25
8      Kp   Red  Hazel    7
9      Kp Black  Black    3
10     Bl Brown  Green   15
11     Bl   Red  Green    7
12     Bl Blond  Brown    4
13     Un Black   Blue    9
14     Un   Red  Hazel    7
15   <NA> Blond   <NA>   NA
```

Helper functions

select has helper functions for selecting columns that are not available in SQL. An example is the contains function helper shown in the following example to select all column that have one or more "e" character in their **names**; hence, eye, gender and freq columns are selected.

```
> select(hec, contains("e"))
   source    eye gender freq
1       Fi Brown   Male   53
2       Fi Brown   Male   10
3       Un Brown   Male    3
4       Fi  Blue   Male   11
5       Kp  Blue Female   30
6       Fi Hazel   Male   10
7       Un Hazel   Male   25
8       Kp Hazel   Male    7
9       Kp Black   Male    3
10      Bl Green   Male   15
11      Bl Green Female    7
12      Bl Brown Female    4
13      Un  Blue Female    9
14      Un Hazel Female    7
15    <NA>  <NA>   <NA>   NA
```

As another example, the following uses the **matches** helper to search column names by regular expression. The .e. means search column names that has any one character followed by "e" and followed by any one character; hence only gender and freq columns are qualified and selected.

```
> select(hec, matches(".e."))
   gender freq
1    Male   53
2    Male   10
3    Male    3
4    Male   11
5  Female   30
6    Male   10
7    Male   25
8    Male    7
9    Male    3
10   Male   15
11 Female    7
12 Female    4
13 Female    9
14 Female    7
15   <NA>   NA
```

By Data Type

You can also select by the data type of the columns. The following select the columns that have numeric data type using the is.numeric helper. hec has only one such column, the freq column (it has a double precision data type to be more precise)

```
> select_if(hec, is.numeric)
    freq
1     53
2     10
3      3
4     11
5     30
6     10
7     25
8      7
9      3
10    15
11     7
12     4
13     9
14     7
15    NA
```

Chapter 5: Ordering Rows

While in SQL's SELECT you use the ORDER BY clause to order the output rows, in dplyr you use the arrange function.

In the following example, the rows are ordered by freq ascending by default.

```
> arrange(hec, freq)
   source  hair    eye gender freq
1      Un Blond  Brown    Male    3
2      Kp Black  Black    Male    3
3      Bl Blond  Brown  Female    4
4      Kp   Red  Hazel    Male    7
5      Bl   Red  Green  Female    7
6      Un   Red  Hazel  Female    7
7      Un Black   Blue  Female    9
8      Fi   Red  Brown    Male   10
9      Fi Black  Hazel    Male   10
10     Fi Black   Blue    Male   11
11     Bl Brown  Green    Male   15
12     Un Brown  Hazel    Male   25
13     Kp Blond   Blue  Female   30
14     Fi Brown  Brown    Male   53
15   <NA> Blond   <NA>    <NA>   NA
```

Descending

The default order is ascending. You can use the desc function
for descending order.

```
> arrange(hec, desc(freq))
   source  hair    eye gender freq
1      Fi Brown  Brown   Male   53
2      Kp Blond   Blue Female   30
3      Un Brown  Hazel   Male   25
4      Bl Brown  Green   Male   15
5      Fi Black   Blue   Male   11
6      Fi   Red  Brown   Male   10
7      Fi Black  Hazel   Male   10
8      Un Black   Blue Female    9
9      Kp   Red  Hazel   Male    7
10     Bl   Red  Green Female    7
11     Un   Red  Hazel Female    7
12     Bl Blond  Brown Female    4
13     Un Blond  Brown   Male    3
14     Kp Black  Black   Male    3
15   <NA> Blond   <NA>   <NA>   NA
```

Multiple columns

To order on multiple columns list the columns in the arrange function's parameter in their ordering hierarchy separated by a comma.

In the following example, we order the output rows by the hair first then freq; meaning if the output rows have more than one rows of the same hair (colour), then the order of these duplicates are by their eye, if they still have duplicates, then they are ordered by gender. For example, the output has two Black hair and Blue eye rows, hence these two rows are ordered by their gender, Female first then Male.

```
> arrange(hec, hair, eye, gender)
   source  hair    eye gender freq
1      Kp Black  Black   Male    3
2      Un Black   Blue Female    9
3      Fi Black   Blue   Male   11
4      Fi Black  Hazel   Male   10
5      Kp Blond   Blue Female   30
6      Bl Blond  Brown Female    4
7      Un Blond  Brown   Male    3
8      Fi Brown  Brown   Male   53
9      Bl Brown  Green   Male   15
10     Un Brown  Hazel   Male   25
11     Fi   Red  Brown   Male   10
12     Bl   Red  Green Female    7
13     Un   Red  Hazel Female    7
14     Kp   Red  Hazel   Male    7
```

Chapter 6: Manipulating Output Columns

Renaming Column

In SQL you rename output column (a.k.a. column aliasing) as follows.

```
SELECT column AS renamed_column, … FROM table;
```

In dplyr, you use the rename function. In the following example we rename hair to hair.colour.

```
> rename(hec, hair.colour = hair)
     source hair.colour    eye gender freq
1        Fi       Brown  Brown   Male   53
2        Fi         Red  Brown   Male   10
3        Un       Blond  Brown   Male    3
4        Fi       Black   Blue   Male   11
5        Kp       Blond   Blue Female   30
6        Fi       Black  Hazel   Male   10
7        Un       Brown  Hazel   Male   25
8        Kp         Red  Hazel   Male    7
9        Kp       Black  Black   Male    3
10       Bl       Brown  Green   Male   15
11       Bl         Red  Green Female    7
12       Bl       Blond  Brown Female    4
13       Un       Black   Blue Female    9
14       Un         Red  Hazel Female    7
15     <NA>       Blond  <NA>   <NA>    NA
```

Renaming more than one column

In the following example, eye is renamed eye.color and n is renamed freq.

```
> rename(hec, hair.colour = hair, sex = gender)
   source hair.colour   eye    sex freq
1      Fi       Brown Brown   Male   53
2      Fi         Red Brown   Male   10
3      Un       Blond Brown   Male    3
4      Fi       Black  Blue   Male   11
5      Kp       Blond  Blue Female   30
6      Fi       Black Hazel   Male   10
7      Un       Brown Hazel   Male   25
8      Kp         Red Hazel   Male    7
9      Kp       Black Black   Male    3
10     Bl       Brown Green   Male   15
11     Bl         Red Green Female    7
12     Bl       Blond Brown Female    4
13     Un       Black  Blue Female    9
14     Un         Red Hazel Female    7
15   <NA>       Blond  <NA>   <NA>   NA
```

Derived Column

In SQL's SELECT we can have a derived (computed) output column.

```
SELECT *, n/100 FROM table;
```

In dplyr we use mutate function to add such a column. In the following example we rename the derived column freq/10 into norm.freq.

```
> mutate(hec, norm.freq = freq/15)
     source  hair    eye gender freq norm.freq
1        Fi Brown  Brown   Male   53 3.5333333
2        Fi   Red  Brown   Male   10 0.6666667
3        Un Blond  Brown   Male    3 0.2000000
4        Fi Black   Blue   Male   11 0.7333333
5        Kp Blond   Blue Female   30 2.0000000
6        Fi Black  Hazel   Male   10 0.6666667
7        Un Brown  Hazel   Male   25 1.6666667
8        Kp   Red  Hazel   Male    7 0.4666667
9        Kp Black  Black   Male    3 0.2000000
10       Bl Brown  Green   Male   15 1.0000000
11       Bl   Red  Green Female    7 0.4666667
12       Bl Blond  Brown Female    4 0.2666667
13       Un Black   Blue Female    9 0.6000000
14       Un   Red  Hazel Female    7 0.4666667
15     <NA> Blond   <NA>   <NA>   NA        NA
```

Functions

You can use functions to derive an output column. dplyr provides quite a number of functions you can apply on the output columns.

The following examples are functions that operate on character, numeric, and date, and na.omit function to omit NA rows.

toupper/tolower

The touppercase converts string to upper cases, tolowercase
to lower cases.

```
> mutate(hec,
+ hair_uppc = toupper(hair))
   source  hair    eye gender  freq hair_uppc
1       Fi Brown Brown    Male    53     BROWN
2       Fi   Red Brown    Male    10       RED
3       Un Blond Brown    Male     3     BLOND
4       Fi Black  Blue    Male    11     BLACK
5       Kp Blond  Blue  Female    30     BLOND
6       Fi Black Hazel    Male    10     BLACK
7       Un Brown Hazel    Male    25     BROWN
8       Kp   Red Hazel    Male     7       RED
9       Kp Black Black    Male     3     BLACK
10      Bl Brown Green    Male    15     BROWN
11      Bl   Red Green  Female     7       RED
12      Bl Blond Brown  Female     4     BLOND
13      Un Black  Blue  Female     9     BLACK
14      Un   Red Hazel  Female     7       RED

> mutate(hec,
+ hair_lowc = tolower(hair))
   source  hair    eye gender  freq hair_lowc
1       Fi Brown Brown    Male    53     brown
2       Fi   Red Brown    Male    10       red
3       Un Blond Brown    Male     3     blond
4       Fi Black  Blue    Male    11     black
5       Kp Blond  Blue  Female    30     blond
6       Fi Black Hazel    Male    10     black
7       Un Brown Hazel    Male    25     brown
8       Kp   Red Hazel    Male     7       red
9       Kp Black Black    Male     3     black
10      Bl Brown Green    Male    15     brown
11      Bl   Red Green  Female     7       red
12      Bl Blond Brown  Female     4     blond
13      Un Black  Blue  Female     9     black
14      Un   Red Hazel  Female     7       red
```

sqrt

sqrt computes the square root of its parameter, which must be numeric.

```
> mutate(hec,
+ freq.sq = sqrt(freq))
    source  hair    eye gender freq  freq.sq
1       Fi Brown  Brown   Male   53 7.280110
2       Fi   Red  Brown   Male   10 3.162278
3       Un Blond  Brown   Male    3 1.732051
4       Fi Black   Blue   Male   11 3.316625
5       Kp Blond   Blue Female   30 5.477226
6       Fi Black  Hazel   Male   10 3.162278
7       Un Brown  Hazel   Male   25 5.000000
8       Kp   Red  Hazel   Male    7 2.645751
9       Kp Black  Black   Male    3 1.732051
10      Bl Brown  Green   Male   15 3.872983
11      Bl   Red  Green Female    7 2.645751
12      Bl Blond  Brown Female    4 2.000000
13      Un Black   Blue Female    9 3.000000
14      Un   Red  Hazel Female    7 2.645751
```

as.character/as.Date

Assume our hec_source data frame has a date column.

```
> hec_source
  source source.name collect.date
1     Fi       Finch   2017-01-01
2     Kp     Kipling   2017-01-10
3     Un       Union   2017-01-20
4     Bl Yonge Bloor   2017-01-30
> str(hec_source)
'data.frame':   4 obs. of  3 variables:
 $ source      : Factor w/ 4 levels "Bl","F
i","Kp",..: 2 3 4 1
 $ source.name : Factor w/ 4 levels "Finch"
,"Kipling",..: 1 2 3 4
 $ collect.date: Date, format: "2017-01-01"
 ...
```

We can convert, using the as.character function, the collect.date column to character data type.

```
> hec_Dc <- mutate(hec_source,
+ Dc = as.character(collect.date))
> str(hec_Dc)
'data.frame':   4 obs. of  4 variables
:
 $ source      : Factor w/ 4 levels "B
l","Fi","Kp",..: 2 3 4 1
 $ source.name : Factor w/ 4 levels "F
inch","Kipling",..: 1 2 3 4
 $ collect.date: Date, format:  ...
 $ Dc          : chr  "2017-01-01" "20
17-01-10" "2017-01-20" "2017-01-30"
```

Using the as.Date function, we can convert the string back to date data type.

```
> mutate(hec_Dc, as.Date(collect.date)) %>% str()
'data.frame':    4 obs. of  5 variables:
 $ source              : Factor w/ 4 levels "Bl"
Fi","Kp",..: 2 3 4 1
 $ source.name         : Factor w/ 4 levels "Fin
","Kipling",..: 1 2 3 4
 $ collect.date        : Date, format:  ...
 $ Dc                  : chr  "2017-01-01" "2017
1-10" "2017-01-20" "2017-01-30"
 $ as.Date(collect.date): Date, format:  ...
```

na.omit

Assume our hec_source data frame has an NA row as follows.

```
> hec_source
  source source.name collect.date
1     Fi       Finch   2017-01-01
2     Kp     Kipling   2017-01-10
3     Un       Union   2017-01-20
4     Bl Yonge Bloor   2017-01-30
5   <NA>        <NA>   2017-01-31
```

We can use the na.omit to remove the NA row.

```
> na.omit(hec_source)
  source source.name collect.date
1     Fi       Finch   2017-01-01
2     Kp     Kipling   2017-01-10
3     Un       Union   2017-01-20
4     Bl Yonge Bloor   2017-01-30
```

cumsum

The following last example uses the cumsum function, which cumulates the freq of all hec's rows.

```
> mutate(hec,cumsum(freq))
   source  hair    eye gender freq cumsum(freq)
1      Fi Brown  Brown   Male   53           53
2      Fi   Red  Brown   Male   10           63
3      Un Blond  Brown   Male    3           66
4      Fi Black   Blue   Male   11           77
5      Kp Blond   Blue Female   30          107
6      Fi Black  Hazel   Male   10          117
7      Un Brown  Hazel   Male   25          142
8      Kp   Red  Hazel   Male    7          149
9      Kp Black  Black   Male    3          152
10     Bl Brown  Green   Male   15          167
11     Bl   Red  Green Female    7          174
12     Bl Blond  Brown Female    4          178
13     Un Black   Blue Female    9          187
14     Un   Red  Hazel Female    7          194
15     Bv   Red  Black   <NA>   NA           NA
```

case_when

In SQL you can have "case" logic as an output column.

```
SELECT columns,
  CASE
    WHEN condition1
    THEN output_value1
    WHEN condition2
    THEN output_value2
    WHEN ...
    ELSE else_value
  END AS output_column
FROM table
WHERE ... ;
```

Its dplyr equivalent is case_when.

```
mutate(dataframe, columns,
       case_when(
       condition1 ~ value1,
       condition2 ~ value2,
       ...
       TRUE ~ else value))
```

Here's an example. The mutated column he_color will be "Bloody hair" when the hair is "Red", else "Nutty eye" when the eye is "Hazel", else "Other".

```
> mutate(hec, he_color = case_when(
+ hec$hair == "Red" ~ "Bloody hair",
+ hec$eye == "Hazel" ~ "Nutty eye",
+ TRUE ~ "Other"))
   source  hair    eye gender freq     he_color
1      Fi Brown  Brown   Male   53        Other
2      Fi   Red  Brown   Male   10  Bloody hair
3      Un Blond  Brown   Male    3        Other
4      Fi Black   Blue   Male   11        Other
5      Kp Blond   Blue Female   30        Other
6      Fi Black  Hazel   Male   10    Nutty eye
7      Un Brown  Hazel   Male   25    Nutty eye
8      Kp   Red  Hazel   Male    7  Bloody hair
9      Kp Black  Black   Male    3        Other
10     Bl Brown  Green   Male   15        Other
11     Bl   Red  Green Female    7  Bloody hair
12     Bl Blond  Brown Female    4        Other
13     Un Black   Blue Female    9        Other
14     Un   Red  Hazel Female    7  Bloody hair
15     Bv   Red  Black   <NA>   NA  Bloody hair
```

The conditions are evaluated in order. If we put the eye condition before the hair condition, the result (he_color column) will be as follows.

```
> mutate(hec, he_color = case_when(
+ hec$eye == "Hazel" ~ "Nutty eye",
+ hec$hair == "Red" ~ "Bloody hair",
+ TRUE ~ "Other"))
   source  hair   eye gender freq     he_color
1      Fi Brown Brown   Male   53        Other
2      Fi   Red Brown   Male   10  Bloody hair
3      Un Blond Brown   Male    3        Other
4      Fi Black  Blue   Male   11        Other
5      Kp Blond  Blue Female   30        Other
6      Fi Black Hazel   Male   10    Nutty eye
7      Un Brown Hazel   Male   25    Nutty eye
8      Kp   Red Hazel   Male    7    Nutty eye
9      Kp Black Black   Male    3        Other
10     Bl Brown Green   Male   15        Other
11     Bl   Red Green Female    7  Bloody hair
12     Bl Blond Brown Female    4        Other
13     Un Black  Blue Female    9        Other
14     Un   Red Hazel Female    7    Nutty eye
15     Bv   Red Black   <NA>   NA  Bloody hair
```

Chapter 7: Grouping and Aggregating Rows

In SQL, to group rows you use a GROUP BY clause.

```
SELECT grouped_columns FROM table GROUP BY
      grouping_columns;
```

In R, you use the dplyr's group_by function. The group_by function creates a data frame of the grouped rows.

```
> group_by(hec, hair)
Source: local data frame [14 x 5]
Groups: hair [4]
```

	source	hair	eye	gender	freq
	\<fctr\>	\<fctr\>	\<fctr\>	\<fctr\>	\<int\>
1	Fi	Brown	Brown	Male	53
2	Fi	Red	Brown	Male	10
3	Un	Blond	Brown	Male	3
4	Fi	Black	Blue	Male	11
5	Kp	Blond	Blue	Female	30
6	Fi	Black	Hazel	Male	10
7	Un	Brown	Hazel	Male	25
8	Kp	Red	Hazel	Male	7
9	Kp	Black	Black	Male	3
10	Bl	Brown	Green	Male	15
11	Bl	Red	Green	Female	7
12	Bl	Blond	Brown	Female	4
13	Un	Black	Blue	Female	9
14	Un	Red	Hazel	Female	7

You can see the effect of the group_by when you apply a summarise function to the grouped rows.

The following example uses the sum function to count the number of Brown eye for each of the hair colors.

```
> group_by(hec, hair) %>%
+ summarise(brown.eye.count =
+ sum(eye == 'Brown'))
# A tibble: 4 × 2
    hair brown.eye.count
  <fctr>          <int>
1  Black              0
2  Blond              2
3  Brown              1
4    Red              1
```

This next example applies the mean summary function.

```
> group_by(hec, hair) %>%
+ summarise(mean.freq = mean(freq))
# A tibble: 4 × 2
    hair mean.freq
  <fctr>     <dbl>
1  Black   8.25000
2  Blond  12.33333
3  Brown  31.00000
4    Red   7.75000
```

Filtering grouped rows

In SQL, we use the HAVING clause to filter (select) the grouped rows.

```
SELECT columns FROM table GROUP BY columns HAVING
        condition;
```

In dplyr, we use the *filter* function.

```
> group_by(hec, hair) %>%
+ summarise(brown.eye.count =
+ sum(eye == 'Brown')) %>%
+ filter(brown.eye.count >= 1)
# A tibble: 3 x 2
      hair brown.eye.count
  <fctr>             <int>
1  Blond                 2
2  Brown                 1
3    Red                 1
```

Chapter 8: Joining Data Frames

You can join two data frames using the various join function.

inner_join

An inner-join function joins two data frames. The join is on the column specified by the by parameter, which in the following example by the source column.

Note that the source column is in the output once only, from the hec dataframe only.

```
> inner_join(hec, hec_source, by = "source")
   source  hair    eye gender freq source.name
1      Fi Brown  Brown   Male   53       Finch
2      Fi   Red  Brown   Male   10       Finch
3      Un Blond  Brown   Male    3       Union
4      Fi Black   Blue   Male   11       Finch
5      Kp Blond   Blue Female   30     Kipling
6      Fi Black  Hazel   Male   10       Finch
7      Un Brown  Hazel   Male   25       Union
8      Kp   Red  Hazel   Male    7     Kipling
9      Kp Black  Black   Male    3     Kipling
10     Bl Brown  Green   Male   15 Yonge Bloor
11     Bl   Red  Green Female    7 Yonge Bloor
12     Bl Blond  Brown Female    4 Yonge Bloor
13     Un Black   Blue Female    9       Union
14     Un   Red  Hazel Female    7       Union
```

Natural Join

An inner-join without the by = joins the data frames by their common column names, which is the source column. This kind of join is also known as natural join.

```
> inner_join(hec, hec_source)
Joining, by = "source"
   source  hair   eye gender freq source.name
1      Fi Brown Brown   Male   53       Finch
2      Fi   Red Brown   Male   10       Finch
3      Un Blond Brown   Male    3       Union
4      Fi Black  Blue   Male   11       Finch
5      Kp Blond  Blue Female   30     Kipling
6      Fi Black Hazel   Male   10       Finch
7      Un Brown Hazel   Male   25       Union
8      Kp   Red Hazel   Male    7     Kipling
9      Kp Black Black   Male    3     Kipling
10     Bl Brown Green   Male   15 Yonge Bloor
11     Bl   Red Green Female    7 Yonge Bloor
12     Bl Blond Brown Female    4 Yonge Bloor
13     Un Black  Blue Female    9       Union
14     Un   Red Hazel Female    7       Union
```

Let's assume that the hec_source's source column is re-named Station.

```
> hec_source <- rename(hec_source,
+ Station = source)
> hec_source
  Station source.name
1      Fi       Finch
2      Kp     Kipling
3      Un       Union
4      Bl Yonge Bloor
```

Then we need to join the data frames by the "source" column to "Station" column as follows, using the by parameter.

```
> inner_join(hec, hec_source,
+ by = c("source" = "Station"))
   source  hair    eye gender freq source.name
1      Fi Brown Brown    Male   53       Finch
2      Fi   Red Brown    Male   10       Finch
3      Un Blond Brown    Male    3       Union
4      Fi Black  Blue    Male   11       Finch
5      Kp Blond  Blue  Female   30     Kipling
6      Fi Black Hazel    Male   10       Finch
7      Un Brown Hazel    Male   25       Union
8      Kp   Red Hazel    Male    7     Kipling
9      Kp Black Black    Male    3     Kipling
10     Bl Brown Green    Male   15 Yonge Bloor
11     Bl   Red Green  Female    7 Yonge Bloor
12     Bl Blond Brown  Female    4 Yonge Bloor
13     Un Black  Blue  Female    9       Union
14     Un   Red Hazel  Female    7       Union
```

If the data frames have more than one common column, and you want to join them by any specific column (not all common columns), then use the "by" parameter to specify the specific columns to join.

Joining Multiple data frames

You can join more than two data frames.

Assume we have a cal data frames as follows.

```
> cal
          dt mth    yr
1 2017-01-01 Jan 2017
2 2017-01-10 Jan 2017
```

Here's an example of joining three data frames. We first join hec to hec_source naturally (on their common source column), then joining their output to the 3rd data frame, the cal, on their dates columns.

```
> inner_join(hec, hec_source) %>%
+ inner_join(cal, by = c("collect.date" = "dt"))
Joining, by = "source"
  source hair   eye gender freq source.name collect.date mth   yr
1     Fi Brown Brown   Male   53       Finch   2017-01-01 Jan 2017
2     Fi   Red Brown   Male   10       Finch   2017-01-01 Jan 2017
3     Fi Black  Blue   Male   11       Finch   2017-01-01 Jan 2017
4     Kp Blond  Blue Female   30     Kipling   2017-01-10 Jan 2017
5     Fi Black Hazel   Male   10       Finch   2017-01-01 Jan 2017
6     Kp   Red Hazel   Male    7     Kipling   2017-01-10 Jan 2017
7     Kp Black Black   Male    3     Kipling   2017-01-10 Jan 2017
```

left_join, right_join, full_join

Similar to SQL, dplyr also provides function for left, right and full joins.

left_join

left_join produces all output rows from the left hand side data frame regardless any match with the right hand side data frame.

Assume the hec_source data frame has an additional row NI that the hec data frame does not have.

```
> hec_source
  Station       source.name
1      Fi             Finch
2      Kp           Kipling
3      Un             Union
4      Bl       Yonge Bloor
5      NI    Not Identified
```

Here's an example of left_join where the left hand side data frame is the hec_source data frame with the NI extra row.

```
> left_join(hec_source, hec, by = c("Station" = "source"))
   Station   source.name  hair    eye gender freq
1       Fi         Finch Brown  Brown   Male   53
2       Fi         Finch   Red  Brown   Male   10
3       Fi         Finch Black   Blue   Male   11
4       Fi         Finch Black  Hazel   Male   10
5       Kp       Kipling Blond   Blue Female   30
6       Kp       Kipling   Red  Hazel   Male    7
7       Kp       Kipling Black  Black   Male    3
8       Un         Union Blond  Brown   Male    3
9       Un         Union Brown  Hazel   Male   25
10      Un         Union Black   Blue Female    9
11      Un         Union   Red  Hazel Female    7
12      Bl  Yonge Bloor Brown  Green   Male   15
13      Bl  Yonge Bloor   Red  Green Female    7
14      Bl  Yonge Bloor Blond  Brown Female    4
15      NI Not Identified  <NA>   <NA>   <NA>   NA
```

right_join

right_join is kind of the opposite of left_join, it produces all output rows from the righthand side data frame regardless any match with the left hand side data frame.

Assume we have a Bv row in the hec data frame. The hec_source does not have Bv.

```
> hec
   source  hair    eye gender freq
1      Fi Brown  Brown   Male   53
2      Fi   Red  Brown   Male   10
3      Un Blond  Brown   Male    3
4      Fi Black   Blue   Male   11
5      Kp Blond   Blue Female   30
6      Fi Black  Hazel   Male   10
7      Un Brown  Hazel   Male   25
8      Kp   Red  Hazel   Male    7
9      Kp Black  Black   Male    3
10     Bl Brown  Green   Male   15
11     Bl   Red  Green Female    7
12     Bl Blond  Brown Female    4
13     Un Black   Blue Female    9
14     Un   Red  Hazel Female    7
15     Bv   Red  Black   <NA>   NA
```

The output of the following example has all rows from the right hand side hec including the Bv; but, not the UI row from the left hand side hec_source data frame, as the hec does not have any UI.

```
> right_join(hec_source, hec, by = c("Station" = "source"))
   Station source.name  hair    eye gender freq
1       Fi       Finch Brown  Brown   Male   53
2       Fi       Finch   Red  Brown   Male   10
3       Un       Union Blond  Brown   Male    3
4       Fi       Finch Black   Blue   Male   11
5       Kp     Kipling Blond   Blue Female   30
6       Fi       Finch Black  Hazel   Male   10
7       Un       Union Brown  Hazel   Male   25
8       Kp     Kipling   Red  Hazel   Male    7
9       Kp     Kipling Black  Black   Male    3
10      Bl Yonge Bloor Brown  Green   Male   15
11      Bl Yonge Bloor   Red  Green Female    7
12      Bl Yonge Bloor Blond  Brown Female    4
13      Un       Union Black   Blue Female    9
14      Un       Union   Red  Hazel Female    7
15      Bv        <NA>   Red  Black   <NA>   NA
```

full_join

full_join returns all row from both side data frames, regardless matching. NI from the hec_source and Bv from the hec are on the output.

```
> full_join(hec_source, hec, by = c("Station" = "source"))
   Station    source.name  hair    eye gender freq
1       Fi         Finch  Brown  Brown    Male   53
2       Fi         Finch    Red  Brown    Male   10
3       Fi         Finch  Black   Blue    Male   11
4       Fi         Finch  Black  Hazel    Male   10
5       Kp       Kipling  Blond   Blue  Female   30
6       Kp       Kipling    Red  Hazel    Male    7
7       Kp       Kipling  Black  Black    Male    3
8       Un         Union  Blond  Brown    Male    3
9       Un         Union  Brown  Hazel    Male   25
10      Un         Union  Black   Blue  Female    9
11      Un         Union    Red  Hazel  Female    7
12      Bl   Yonge Bloor  Brown  Green    Male   15
13      Bl   Yonge Bloor    Red  Green  Female    7
14      Bl   Yonge Bloor  Blond  Brown  Female    4
15      NI Not Identified  <NA>   <NA>    <NA>   NA
16      Bv                 <NA>    Red   Black   <NA>   NA
```

Chapter 9: Combining Data Frames

Just like in SQL, in R you can also combine multiple data frames of the same structure into one data frame using the dplyr's union_all, union, intersect, and setdiff function.

Assume we have the following cal and cal.more data frames. The two data frames have the same structure. Note that both have "2017-01-10".

```
> cal
          dt mth   yr
1 2017-01-01 Jan 2017
2 2017-01-10 Jan 2017
> cal.more
          dt mth   yr
1 2017-01-10 Jan 2017
2 2017-01-15 Jan 2017
3 2017-01-20 Jan 2017
4 2017-01-30 Jan 2017
5 2017-01-31 Jan 2017
```

union_all

union_all combines all rows into one data frame, including
the two same "2017-01-10" rows.

```
> union_all(cal, cal.more)
          dt mth    yr
1 2017-01-01 Jan 2017
2 2017-01-10 Jan 2017
3 2017-01-10 Jan 2017
4 2017-01-15 Jan 2017
5 2017-01-20 Jan 2017
6 2017-01-30 Jan 2017
7 2017-01-31 Jan 2017
```

union

union combines all rows from the two data frames, but
duplicates are removed; the resulting data frame has only one
"2017-01-10"

```
> union(cal, cal.more)
          dt mth    yr
1 2017-01-20 Jan 2017
2 2017-01-10 Jan 2017
3 2017-01-31 Jan 2017
4 2017-01-15 Jan 2017
5 2017-01-01 Jan 2017
6 2017-01-30 Jan 2017
```

intersect

intersect-ing two data frames produce a data frame from their common rows. In the following example, the two data frames have one common row only, the "2017-01-10".

```
> intersect(cal.more, cal)
          dt mth    yr
1 2017-01-10 Jan 2017
```

setdiff

setdiff produces a data frame containing the rows from the left hand side data frame that are not in the right hand side data frame.

```
> setdiff(cal.more, cal)
          dt mth    yr
1 2017-01-15 Jan 2017
2 2017-01-20 Jan 2017
3 2017-01-30 Jan 2017
4 2017-01-31 Jan 2017
```

If we switch the position of the data frames, the resulting data frame is now only the "2017-01-01" row from the cal that is not in the cal.more.

```
> setdiff(cal, cal.more)
          dt mth    yr
1 2017-01-01 Jan 2017
```

bind_rows

Additionally, dplyr has the bind_rows function. It is similar to union_all, but you can request it to add a column to identify the source data frame of the rows by providing the .id parameter.

```
> bind_rows("cal"= cal,
+ "cal.more"= cal.more,
+ .id = "data.frame")
  data.frame          dt mth   yr
1        cal 2017-01-01 Jan 2017
2        cal 2017-01-10 Jan 2017
3   cal.more 2017-01-10 Jan 2017
4   cal.more 2017-01-15 Jan 2017
5   cal.more 2017-01-20 Jan 2017
6   cal.more 2017-01-30 Jan 2017
7   cal.more 2017-01-31 Jan 2017
```

Chapter 10: View

In SQL database, a view is effectively a predefined query. You create a view using the CREATE VIEW statement.

```
CREATE VIEW view_name (columns) AS SELECT ... ;
```

The SELECT ... statement is the predefined query.

Once you have a view created, when you use it the predefined query is executed. You use a view just like it's a table (hence a view is a.k.a. virtual table)

One way to implement a view in R is by creating a function that defines the predefined query. Here's an example with a simple predefined query using the mutate function.

```
> hec_view1 <- function() {
+ mutate(hec, norm.freq = freq/10)}
```

When used (called) the hec_view1 function will execute the predefined query and return resulting rows.

```
> hec_view1()
   source  hair    eye gender freq norm.freq
1      Fi Brown  Brown   Male   53       5.3
2      Fi   Red  Brown   Male   10       1.0
3      Un Blond  Brown   Male    3       0.3
4      Fi Black   Blue   Male   11       1.1
5      Kp Blond   Blue Female   30       3.0
6      Fi Black  Hazel   Male   10       1.0
7      Un Brown  Hazel   Male   25       2.5
8      Kp   Red  Hazel   Male    7       0.7
9      Kp Black  Black   Male    3       0.3
10     Bl Brown  Green   Male   15       1.5
11     Bl   Red  Green Female    7       0.7
12     Bl Blond  Brown Female    4       0.4
13     Un Black   Blue Female    9       0.9
14     Un   Red  Hazel Female    7       0.7
15   <NA> Blond   <NA>   <NA>   NA        NA
```

Just like in SQL database where you can use a view as if it's a table, hec_view1 can be used as if it's just a data frame. In the following example we use the hec_view1 as a data frame parameter of the filter function.

```
> filter(hec_view1(), hair == "Red")
   source hair    eye gender freq norm.freq
1      Fi  Red  Brown   Male   10       1.0
2      Kp  Red  Hazel   Male    7       0.7
3      Bl  Red  Green Female    7       0.7
4      Un  Red  Hazel Female    7       0.7
```

Nested View

A view can be based on another view. Such a view is called a nested view.

In the following example, the hec_view11 has inside it the previously created hec_view1.

```
> hec_view11 <- function() {
+ filter(hec_view1(), hair == 'Red')}
> hec_view11()
  source hair    eye gender freq norm.freq
1     Fi  Red  Brown   Male   10       1.0
2     Kp  Red  Hazel   Male    7       0.7
3     Bl  Red  Green Female    7       0.7
4     Un  Red  Hazel Female    7       0.7
```

Note that a view does not store the resulting output rows, meaning, when you use a view its predefined query will run against the data at that time. We can say that a view is dynamic: the returned rows can be different when data frame changes over the period.

Lastly, a view is especially useful, in particular those with complex pre-defined query, when you will/need to re-use it.

Chapter 11: Sub-query

In SQL you can nest a query within query. In R you can do similarly as shown in the following example where we nest a mutate query inside a filter query.

```
> filter(
+ mutate(hec, norm.freq = freq/10),
+ hair == "Red")
  source hair   eye gender freq norm.freq
1     Fi Red Brown   Male   10       1.0
2     Kp Red Hazel   Male    7       0.7
3     Bl Red Green Female    7       0.7
4     Un Red Hazel Female    7       0.7
```

In this example, we effectively feed the resulting data frame from the mutate function as the parameter of the filter function.

Not all kind of dplyr queries can be nested this way. A better alternative is to use the pipe %>%.

```
> mutate(hec, norm.freq = freq/10) %>%
+ filter(hair == "Red")
  source hair   eye gender freq norm.freq
1     Fi Red Brown   Male   10       1.0
2     Kp Red Hazel   Male    7       0.7
3     Bl Red Green Female    7       0.7
4     Un Red Hazel Female    7       0.7
```

Chapter 12: Maintaining Data

dplyr offers functions to add, update and delete data in a data frame.

Adding Rows

To add rows use the add_row function.

The following example add a row (Sc, Scarborough) to the hec_source data frame.

```
> hec_source <- add_row(hec_source,
+ source = 'Sc',
+ source.name = 'Scarborough')
> hec_source
  source source.name
1     Fi        Finch
2     Kp      Kipling
3     Un        Union
4     Bl  Yonge Bloor
5     Sc  Scarborough
```

Here's an example of adding multiple rows.

```
> hec_source <- add_row(hec_source,
+ source = c('Kn', 'Du'),
+ source.name = c('Kennedy', 'Dundas'))
> hec_source
  source source.name
1     Fi        Finch
2     Kp      Kipling
3     Un        Union
4     Bl  Yonge Bloor
5     Sc  Scarborough
6     Kn      Kennedy
7     Du       Dundas
```

Updating Rows

Use the mutate with the if_else function to update specific rows.

In the following example, we update rows with 'Fi' to 'Fn'.

Before

```
> hec_source
    source source.name collect.date
1      Fi         Finch   2017-01-01
2      Kp       Kipling   2017-01-10
3      Un         Union   2017-01-20
4      Bl   Yonge Bloor   2017-01-30
```

the update

```
> hec_source <- mutate(hec_source,
+ source = if_else(source == 'Fi', 'Fn',
+ as.character(source)))
```

after

```
> hec_source
    source source.name collect.date
1      Fn         Finch   2017-01-01
2      Kp       Kipling   2017-01-10
3      Un         Union   2017-01-20
4      Bl   Yonge Bloor   2017-01-30
```

Deleting Rows

You can use filter with the not operator ! to delete rows.

The following example deletes Fn and Bl rows from the hec_source data frame.

```
> hec_source <- filter(hec_source,
+ ! source %in% c('Fn', 'Bl'))
> hec_source
  source source.name collect.date
1     Kp     Kipling   2017-01-10
2     Un       Union   2017-01-20
```

Index

www.ingramcontent.com/pod-product-compliance
Lightning Source LLC
Chambersburg PA
CBHW061030050326
40689CB00012B/2748